MW01700884

The Big Book of SILLY JOKES FOR KIDS

I tried to write with a broken pencil... but it made no point.

Why did the gift wear sunglasses?

It was wrapped in style.

What can you catch but not throw?

A cold.

Why did the cookie blush?

Because it saw the frosting.

How do you make a test less scary?

Take a deep breath and do your best.

Why did the knight bring a notebook?

To take notes in shining armor.

Why did the pirate carry a bar of soap?

To wash up on shore.

Knock, knock.
Who's there?
Luke.
Luke who?
Luke at the time - it's snack o'clock!

Why did the cookie go to the doctor?

Because it felt crummy.

What do you call a whale that tells jokes?

A pun-whale.

Why did the student bring a ladder to school?

Because they wanted to go to high school.

Knock, knock.
Who's there?
Spell.
Spell who?
Okay: W-H-O!

What do you call a turtle that takes selfies?

A shell-fie star.

What can be opened but isn't a door?

A book.

What do you call a penguin in the desert?

Lost.

Knock, knock.
Who's there?
Dew.
Dew who?
Dew you have any snacks?

Knock, knock.
Who's there?
Snow.
Snow who?
Snow use - I forgot my key!

Why did the broccoli feel important?

It was a little tree-mendous.

What do you call a duck on a bicycle?

A quack in the saddle.

What do you call a planet that can dance?

A disco-very.

Knock, knock.
Who's there?
Muffin.
Muffin who?
Muffin much - what's up with you?

Why did the turtle bring a backpack?

It liked to carry its home with it.

What do you call an octopus that can read?

A well-armed reader.

I asked a snowman for advice.
He said, 'Just chill.'

Why did the hamster run in its wheel?

It was chasing its dreams.

What has a face and two hands but no arms or legs?

A clock.

Why did the bee get good grades?

It always did its buzz-iness.

Goofy geese glided 5 glittery grapes.

Why did the plate feel nervous?

It was afraid of being judged.

Why did the baseball glove feel proud?

It made a great catch.

How do you make a monkey stop monkeying around?

Give it a banana-bribe.

What do you call a peacock that loves to brag?

A show-off feather.

What do you call a sleeping puppy?

A napper-dog.

What do you call a snowman who tells jokes?

A chill comedian.

Knock, knock.
Who's there?
Yo.
Yo who?
Yo-yo! I'm bouncing in to say hi!

What do you call a bear that loves birthdays?

A party bear.

Why did the snowflake smile?

It was one of a kind.

Why did the glue stick around?

Because it was attached to its friends.

How do you make a spoon stop being grumpy?

Stir in some smiles.

Knock, knock.
Who's there?
Wendy.
Wendy who?
Wendy you open the door already?

How do you make a sandwich stop being shy?

Tell it to come out of its shell (wrap).

Why did the comedian bring a ladder?

To take the jokes to the next level.

How do you make a computer snack?

Give it micro-chips.

What do you call a book that is full of jokes?

A giggle-ography.

Why did the ruler feel confident?

It always measured up.

Knock, knock.
Who's there?
Atch.
Atch who?
Bless you!

How do you make a cup feel cheerful?

Fill it with good news.

What do you call a fish that loves school?

A straight-A tuna.

Why did the rainbow smile?

It had all the right colors (in its imagination).

Why did the lunchbox feel excited?

Because it had a surprise inside.

What do you call an astronaut who is messy?

A space cadet.

Why did the grapes giggle?

They heard a grape joke.

How do you make an octopus laugh?

With ten-tickles.

Why did the grape stop in the middle of the road?

Because it ran out of juice.

Mysterious moons mumbled 9 messy magicians.

Mellow milkshakes mooned 9 merry monkeys.

What do you call a dog in the sun?

A hot dog.

What do you call a duck that loves telling jokes?

A wise quacker.

What has a spine but never stands up?

A book.

Tippy toasters tested 6 tropical tacos.

Knock, knock.
Who's there?
Hope.
Hope who?
Hope you have a great day!

Why did the pig bring a suitcase?

It was going on a hogiday.

Why did the leaf go to school?

To turn over a new page.

I ate a clock once...
it was very time-consuming.

The broom got promoted.
It really swept everyone away.

What do you call a cat that loves to read?

A book-purr.

Why did the backpack look stressed?

It had too much baggage.

I bought a dinosaur dictionary. It was a thesaurus.

What do you call a lobster that loves jokes?

A pun-ster lobster.

What do you call a bear that can't stop complaining?

Un-bear-able.

What has one eye but can't see?

A needle.

How do you make an apple smile?

Tell it it's the core of the team.

Dizzy dinosaurs drummed 9 dizzy dolls.

What do you call a cookie that can sing?

A sweet-tooth star.

What do you call a rabbit that tells jokes?

A funny bunny.

Why did the banana sit on the floor?

It wanted to be a slippery joke.

How do you make a mop feel useful?

Let it clean up the mess-tery.

Why did the calendar look worried?

Because its days were numbered.

What do you call a cat who is a great musician?

A purr-cussionist.

Marvelous milkshakes measured 4 muddy masks.

Knock, knock.
Who's there?
May I.
May I who?
May I come in?

What do you call a turkey after a joke?

A giggle-gobbler.

Why did the ocean feel friendly?

It waved.

What do you call a bear that loves coffee?

A bearista.

How do you make a tissue dance?

Put a little boogie in it.

How do you make a bicycle faster?

Cheer it on and give it a little push.

Why did the teddy bear say no to dessert?

Because it was stuffed.

What do you call a robot that loves taking baths?

A scrub-bot.

How do you make a banana split?

Tell it a really funny joke.

How do you make scissors feel safe?

Give them a snug holder.

Why did the shoe go to school?

To become a little smarter (and tie things together).

Why did the eraser feel proud?

It fixed a big mistake.

What do you call a banana that's really brave?

A hero-peel.

Why did the musician bring a ladder?

To reach the high notes.

Tangled teapots tiptoed 8 talkative tigers.

What gets bigger the more you take away?

A hole.

Brave bees bounced 7 brave bananas.

Why did the wizard love the library?

It was full of spell-binding books.

How do you make a giraffe feel included?

Say hi from way up there.

My suitcase is always hungry. It keeps packing snacks.

Why did the pencil go to the principal?

It got in trouble for drawing in class.

Watery wheels waved 3 whispery worms.

What has a head and a tail but no body?

A coin.

What do you call a robot that loves art?

A doodle-droid.

Why did the panda bring sunglasses?

It was too cool for bamboo.

How do you make a lion laugh?

Tell it a roaring good joke.

Why did the pencil cross the page?

To get to the other line.

Knock, knock.
Who's there?
Dew.
Dew who?
Dew you like jokes as much as I do?

What can jump higher than a house?

Anything - houses can't jump.

What gets wetter the more it dries?

A towel.

Why did the owl bring a map?

It didn't want to get lost in the hoo-dini act.

Why did the fork sit next to the spaghetti?

It wanted to stick around.

How do you make grapes stop arguing?

Tell them to let it go and wine later.

What has a tail but no legs and likes to fly?

A kite.

What do you call a ruler that tells jokes?

A funny measure.

How do you make a computer happy?

Give it a good byte to eat.

What do you call a rabbit that works in an office?

A hare assistant.

Knock, knock.
Who's there?
Owls.
Owls who?
Yes, they do!

What do you call a marker that loves attention?

A highlight.

How do you catch a squirrel?

Climb a tree and act like a nut!

Clever cats cooked 7 crunchy cupcakes.

How do you make a panda relax?

Let it bamboo-lieve everything will be okay.

What is orange and sounds like a parrot?

A carrot.

How do you make a stapler feel useful?

Give it a big stack to tackle.

Why did the paper airplane feel proud?

It really flew through the test.

How do you make a toothbrush feel brave?

Tell it to face the plaque.

Why did the cloud go to school?

To learn how to make better shapes.

Why did the banana go out with the prune?

Because it couldn't find a date.

How do you help a flower grow?

Give it a little encouragement (and sunshine!).

How do you make a shirt feel fancy?

Give it a bow tie.

Why did the marker feel bold?

Because it liked to stand out.

Funny flowers flew 4 fearless feathers.

What can you break even if you never pick it up?

A promise.

What do you call a sleepy astronaut?

An astro-napper.

Wacky worms whistled 3 watery wolves.

Why did the train stop at the station?

It had to let off some steam.

Knock, knock.
Who's there?
Cow says.
Cow says who?
No silly - cow says 'moo'!

How do you make a llama stop being dramatic?

Tell it, 'No prob-llama!'

Why did the book bring a flashlight?

To read under the covers.

What do you call a snowman who tells tall stories?

A frosty fibber.

Knock, knock.
Who's there?
Ivy.
Ivy who?
Ivy been waiting forever!

What do you call cheese that isn't yours?

Nacho cheese.

Knock, knock.
Who's there?
Olive.
Olive who?
Olive the snacks disappeared!

What has four fingers and a thumb but can't hold a pencil?

A glove.

The cookie went to school.
It wanted to be a smart cookie.

Why did the spoon sit in the soup?

It wanted to be in the mix.

Knock, knock.
Who's there?
Icy.
Icy who?
Icy you peeking!

How do you make a mushroom feel welcome?

Tell it there's always room for it.

Why did the fridge feel popular?

Everyone kept visiting it.

How do you make a cow stop complaining?

Tell it to mooo-ve on.

What can fill a room but takes up no space?

Light.

Why did the balloon feel happy?

Because it was on the rise.

Friendly foxes frolicked 7 fast fries.

What do you call an otter that loves jokes?

An otterly funny friend.

Why did the pirate love the alphabet?

Because it had lots of 'arrs' and 'seas'.

What has stripes and goes 'zzz'?

A sleeping zebra.

Why did the sheep bring a pencil?

It wanted to draw a baa-rilliant picture.

How do you make pizza feel special?

Give it a big slice of attention.

What do you call a zebra that tells jokes?

A stripe comedian.

Knock, knock.
Who's there?
Robin.
Robin who?
Robin you a big hug!

How do you make a duck pay attention?

Give it a quack-tion.

Why did the plate sit in the sun?

It wanted to be a hot dish.

Why did the snowman look in the fridge?

It was hoping to chill out.

Why did the magnet get invited to the party?

Because it was so attractive.

Why did the cup join the choir?

It loved to sing with a full voice.

Why did the rabbit eat a carrot?

It wanted some hare-raising crunch.

Why did the golfer bring two pairs of pants?

In case he got a hole in one.

What do you call a pencil that tells jokes?

A pun-cil.

Knock, knock.
Who's there?
A bee.
A bee who?
A bee-cause I wanted to say hi!

How do you make a clock laugh?
Tell it a timed joke.

Knock, knock.
Who's there?
Boo hoo.
Boo hoo who?
Don't cry - I brought cookies!

What do you call a lion that tells jokes?
A roar comedian.

Knock, knock.
Who's there?
Ya-hoo.
Ya-hoo who?
I prefer 'you'!

What do you call a snowman party?
A snow-ball.

Why did the horse sit at the computer?
It wanted to surf the web.

How do you make a skateboard stop wobbling?
Tighten it up and keep rolling.

Why did the dolphin bring a suitcase?

It was going on a fin-tastic trip.

Why did the cup feel brave?

It was full of courage (and cocoa).

What do you call a penguin with a great singing voice?

An ice-pop star.

Why did the melon have a big wedding?

Because it cantaloupe!

Why did the cow become an artist?

It loved to draw mooo-dels.

I asked the lamp to be quiet.
It said, 'Sorry, I get bright ideas!'

Why did the math book look sad?

Because it had too many problems.

What do you call a bear caught in the rain?

A drizzly bear.

Why did the shirt join the band?

It wanted to be part of the crew-neck.

What do you call a dinosaur that loves candy?

A sweet-osaurus.

Why did the mushroom get invited to the party?

Because it was a fungi.

Why did the apple join the band?

Because it had great core-dination.

Knock, knock.
Who's there?
Dewey.
Dewey who?
Dewey have to clean my room?

What do you call a sleeping dinosaur?

A dino-snore.

What do you call a dinosaur that loves tacos?

A snack-osaurus.

Sparkly snowmen smiled 3 shiny spoons.

How do you make ice cream calm down?

Tell it to chill.

Why did the lamp get grounded?

It couldn't stop light-ing up.

What do you call a sheep that loves selfies?

A baa-rilliant influencer.

How do you make a crayon feel artistic?

Let it color outside the lines.

Why did the camera blink?

It saw something picture-perfect.

Why did the dinosaur bring a map?

It didn't want to get lost in prehistory.

What has to be broken before you can use it?

An egg.

Why did the stapler get promoted?

It really held things together.

How do you make a calculator smile?

Give it something to count on.

What do you call a bee that loves school?

A study bee.

What is as light as a feather but even the strongest person can't hold it for long?

Your breath.

Why did the dinosaur sit on the egg?

It wanted to hatch a plan.

What has a tail and a head and is used to pay?

A coin.

Knock, knock.
Who's there?
Ben.
Ben who?
Ben waiting forever!

What do you call a fish that loves jokes?

Finny.

How do you make a spoon feel included?

Invite it to the scoop.

Why did the drummer bring snacks?

It wanted to keep the beat and eat.

Knock, knock.
Who's there?
Woo.
Woo who?
Don't get too excited - it's just me!

Knock, knock.
Who's there?
Minnie.
Minnie who?
Minnie more minutes and I'll leave!

How do you make a ghost smile?

Say 'Boo-tiful!'

Knock, knock.
Who's there?
Honeydew.
Honeydew who?
Honeydew you know how sweet you are?

Little llamas looped 6 lazy lions.

How do you make a cat stop interrupting?

Ask it to paws and listen.

Knock, knock.
Who's there?
Alpaca.
Alpaca who?
Alpaca lunch for our picnic!

What do you call a shark that plays music?

A great white rapper.

Knock, knock.
Who's there?
Dewey.
Dewey who?
Dewey have to do homework?

Knock, knock.
Who's there?
Boo-berry.
Boo-berry who?
Boo-berry nice to meet you!

What do you call a dolphin that loves school?

Smarty-fins.

How do you make a turtle hurry?

You don't - you just cheer it on!

What do you call a dog that works at a bakery?

A dough-berman.

What do you call a penguin that tells jokes?

A comedi-hen.

What do you call a chicken at the playground?

A swing-wing.

How do you get a robot to relax?

Tell it to reboot and chill.

Why did the mountain sit still?

It didn't want to peak too soon.

Why did the robot bring a snack?

It needed fuel for its funny circuits.

Knock, knock.
Who's there?
Lettuce.
Lettuce who?
Lettuce in - it's cold out here!

Knock, knock.
Who's there?
Who.
Who who?
Okay, owl admit it - that's funny.

What do you call a sleeping dictionary?

A nap-tionary.

How do you fix a broken tomato?

Tomato paste!

What can you put between a fork and a spoon?

The word 'and'.

Knock, knock.
Who's there?
Harry.
Harry who?
Harry up - it's snack time!

Why did the broom bring a friend?

Because it liked to sweep in pairs.

Why did the cookie go to the gym?

To get into chip-top shape.

What do you call a bear in a party hat?

A cele-bear-tion.

Why did the orange bring a jacket?

It didn't want to catch a peel-ing cold.

Puffy penguins paddled 8 purple pizzas.

What has keys but can't open locks?

A piano.

Why did the toothbrush go to the party?

It wanted to brush up on jokes.

Lively lions lingered 3 loud ladybugs.

Purple pizzas pranced 8 plucky puppies.

What do you call a llama that tells jokes?

A laugh-a-llama.

Why did the banana go to the doctor?

It wasn't peeling well.

What do you call scissors that tell jokes?

A cut-up.

How do you make a moon laugh?

Tell it a cheesy joke.

Why did the chicken cross the road?

To get to the other side.

My pizza told me a joke... it was pretty cheesy.

How do you make a noodle laugh?

Say something im-pasta-bly funny.

What has a horn but doesn't honk?

A rhinoceros.

How do you make a taco stop falling apart?

Hold it together!

The cereal started singing. It was a bowl-d performer!

What has legs but doesn't walk?

A table.

What do you call a sheep with no legs?

A cloud.

Whispery windows whistled 9 whispery wolves.

How do you make a pirate smile?

Say, 'Aye, matey!'

Why did the basketball go to school?

It wanted to learn how to bounce back.

How do you make a pillow feel important?

Give it the top spot on the bed.

What kind of music do balloons hate?

Pop music.

Knock, knock.
Who's there?
Ice.
Ice who?
Ice to meet you!

What comes down but never goes up?

Rain.

I'm reading a book about anti-gravity. It's impossible to put down!

What do you call a cow in an earthquake?

A milkshake.

What do you call a frog that parks illegally?

Toad.

Why did the scarecrow win an award?

Because he was outstanding in his field.

What do you call an owl that can sing?

A hoot-star.

What do you call a pirate who loves music?

A sea-shanty fan.

Knock, knock.
Who's there?
Cheetah.
Cheetah who?
Cheetah peek - open up!

Loopy lollipops laughed 4 lively lions.

What do you call a camel that loves games?

A hump-day champion.

Wide windows wobbled 3 watery waffles.

Knock, knock.
Who's there?
Fur.
Fur who?
Fur goodness' sake, open the door!

What do you call a duck that gets all A's?

A wise quacker.

How do you make a shoe tell the truth?

Ask it to be laced with honesty.

What do you call a cow that cuts the grass?

A lawn mooer.

What do you call a notebook that can sing?

A note-book.

What do you call a robot that tells bedtime stories?

A tale-bot.

How do you make a snake smile?

Tell it something hiss-terical.

What has lots of branches but no leaves?

A bank.

I told the ocean a joke.
It just waved.

What do you call a crayon that feels important?

A big deal marker.

Why did the lamp feel important?

It had bright ideas.

Why did the crayon stay in the box?

It didn't want to draw attention.

Why did the astronaut bring a pencil to space?

To draw the moon.

Why did the bicycle fall over?

Because it was two-tired.

Why did the stapler bring a helmet?

It was ready for a paper jam.

Fancy fries flew 3 fancy fireflies.

Why did the dragon eat a candle?

It wanted a light snack.

How do you make a hamster feel like a hero?

Give it a tiny cape.

How do you make a cupcake feel special?

Give it extra sprinkles.

Why did the ghost bring a suitcase?

It was going on a fright trip.

How do you make a balloon feel brave?

Tell it not to be afraid to rise.

Why did the sandwich bring a ladder?

It wanted to make a bigger sub.

Knock, knock.
Who's there?
Robin.
Robin who?
Robin you of a hug!

Why did the elephant bring a suitcase to the zoo?

It heard there were lots of trunks.

How do you make a rabbit calm down?

Tell it to hop off the worry.

I tried to catch fog yesterday... I mist.

What has a heart but no other organs?
A deck of cards.

Fearless fans fizzed 3 fuzzy fries.

How do you make a fork feel helpful?
Tell it to stick with you.

Why did the owl get invited to every party?
Because it was a hoot.

What has ears but can't hear?
Corn.

Knock, knock.
Who's there?
Goliath.
Goliath who?
Goliath down - I'm trying to sleep!

Why did the robot go to school?
To improve its class-mates.

What can you find in the middle of nowhere?

The letter H.

What do you call a very tiny joke?

A puny pun.

Why did the artist bring a pencil?

To draw attention.

Why did the crayon quit?

It felt like it was being worn down.

Knock, knock.
Who's there?
Cereal.
Cereal who?
Cereal-ously, let me in!

What do you call a dinosaur that loves to draw?

An art-osaurus.

How do you make a fork feel brave?

Tell it to take the plunge (into pasta).

What has a neck but no head?

A bottle.

Why did the pirate go to school?

To improve his arrr-ticulation.

Why did the donut go to the dentist?

It needed a filling.

How do you throw a party in space?

You planet.

Knock, knock.
Who's there?
Hazel.
Hazel who?
Hazel-nut you open the door?

Why did the paper bring a sweater?

It was feeling a little sheet-y.

What can travel around the world while staying in a corner?

A stamp.

Sneaky stars squeaked 8 sticky spoons.

What do you call an elephant that can fly?

A jumbo jet.

What do you call a cat who works at a school?

A purr-fessor.

Why did the fish blush?

Because it saw the ocean's bottom.

Knock, knock.
Who's there?
Beets.
Beets who?
Beets me - I forgot my keys!

What is full of holes but still holds water?

A sponge.

Knock, knock.
Who's there?
Annie.
Annie who?
Annie-one up for a game?

How do you make a bee laugh?

Tell it a buzz-tingly funny joke.

What do you call a bee that is really smart?

A spelling bee.

I tried to make a belt out of watches.
It was a waist of time.

How do you make a fridge feel popular?

Keep opening it for snacks!

What can you throw but never catch?

A party.

What has an endless supply of letters but starts empty?

A mailbox.

Knock, knock.
Who's there?
Theo.
Theo who?
Theo only way in is through this door!

Why did the marker go to art class?

It wanted to make a bold statement.

I wanted to be a train driver, but I lost my track.

Knock, knock.
Who's there?
Ewe.
Ewe who?
Ewe are so funny!

Why did the ice cream truck break down?

It had a rocky road.

Why did the monster eat a clock?

It was time for a snack.

How do you make an alien feel at home?

Welcome it to planet Earth.

What do you call a cat in a fancy suit?

Fur-mal.

Why did the frog bring a notebook?

To write down ribbiting ideas.

What do you call a turtle that loves jokes?

A shell-arious pal.

Knock, knock.
Who's there?
I scream.
I scream who?
I scream because you won't let me in!

Why did the moon stay up late?

It couldn't stop waxing poetic.

What kind of band never plays music?

A rubber band.

What kind of dog keeps the best time?

A watch-dog.

Why did the teacher wear sunglasses?

Because the students were so bright.

The robot told a joke. It was totally bolt-astic.

What do you call a giraffe with a short neck?

A deer.

Why did the muffin hide?

It was feeling a little crumb-y.

How do you make a frog start a band?

Add a few ribbiting instruments.

Knock, knock.
Who's there?
Toad.
Toad who?
Toad-ally awesome to see you!

What do you call a koala that loves the computer?

A koalafied coder.

Knock, knock.
Who's there?
Liam.
Liam who?
Liam on the doorbell!

What do you call a bunny after it tells a joke?

A funny hare.

What is so fragile that saying its name breaks it?

Silence.

What do you call a pencil that's always late?

Behind schedule.

What do you call a mouse that likes to cook?

A chef squeak.

How do you make a lemon drop?

Just let it fall.

Knock, knock.
Who's there?
Elle.
Elle who?
Elle you later!

What has a bottom at the top?

Your legs.

What do you call a frog that loves jokes?

A ribbiting comedian.

Why did the glue stay calm?

It knew how to stick with it.

What goes up but never comes down?

Your age.

What do you call a book about mountains?

Cliff Notes.

Why did the kite go to school?

To learn how to soar.

Cheerful crayons clapped 9 clever clouds.

How do you make a bus blush?

Give it lots of compliments on its route.

Why did the balloon bring a friend?

It didn't want to pop in alone.

I used to be a baker, but I couldn't make enough dough.

What do you call a cat that loves to paint?
An art-purr.

What do you call a wizard who loves snacks?
A munch-ician.

What can you see in water but never get wet?
Your reflection.

What has letters but never goes to the post office?
The alphabet.

What do you call a pig that knows karate?
pork chop.

Why did the scientist bring a ladder?
To reach new heights in learning.

Why did the octopus laugh?
Because it was well-armed with jokes.

What do you call a dinosaur that loves jokes?
A dino-mite comedian.

What do you call a cat who loves to go camping?
A purr-scout.

Why did the notebook go to the party?
It wanted to take notes on the fun.

What do you call a can opener that doesn't work?
A can't opener.

What do you call a boomerang that doesn't come back?
A stick.

How do you make a magnet laugh?
Tell it something attractive.

How do you make a kite feel proud?
Let it fly high.

Why did the pirate bring a pencil?
To draw his treasure map.

What kind of tree can you carry in your hand?

A palm.

Why did the skateboard blush?

It got caught rolling around.

Why did the apple stop rolling down the hill?

It ran out of core-age.

The computer sneezed... it had a little virus.

I told my backpack a joke. It couldn't handle it.

What do you call a monkey that loves potato chips?

A chip-munk.

Why did the paperclip smile?

It was holding everything together.

Knock, knock.
Who's there?
Boo.
Boo who?
Don't cry - it's just a joke!

Knock, knock.
Who's there?
Luke.
Luke who?
Luke, I brought cookies!

How do you make a cloud stop following you?
Walk under a rainbow.

The pencil was broken...
so it felt pretty pointless.

Why did the cat bring a suitcase?
It was going on a purr-fect vacation.

What kind of coat is always wet when you put it on?
A coat of paint.

Why did the bus bring a blanket?
It was going on a long ride.

What is always in front of you but can't be seen?
The future.

How do you make soap feel successful?
Let it clean up its act.

Why did the singer bring a ladder to practice?

To climb the charts.

Giant grapes gobbled 8 giant ghosts.

What do you call a seal that loves music?

A seal-ebrities band.

Knock, knock.
Who's there?
Brrr.
Brrr who?
Brrr - it's cold! Let me in!

Why did the party hat wobble?

It was having a good time.

What do you call an octopus that loves hugs?

A snuggle-pus.

Speedy squirrels spun 9 sparkly sandwiches.

What do you call a planet that sings?

Nept-tune.

What do you call a robot that loves to skateboard?

A roll-bot.

Watery windows winked 8 watery worms.

How do you make a monster friendly?

Offer it a high-five and a cookie.

My alarm clock is so dramatic. It always makes a big scene in the morning.

What do you call a snail that rides a turtle?

A slowpoke.

Knock, knock.
Who's there?
Aloha.
Aloha who?
Aloha lot - open up!

Drowsy ducks dribbled 5 dramatic donuts.

Busy bagels buzzed 5 busy bananas.

What do you call a snail that runs fast?

A miracle.

What do you call a cow with one leg?

Steak.

What do you call a happy piece of bread?

A loaf with a grin.

Knock, knock.
Who's there?
Art.
Art who?
Art you ready for a joke?

How do you make a teacher smile?

Use kind words and good manners.

I tried to play hide-and-seek with a mountain.
It was always peak-a-boo!

How do you make a marker feel bold?

Tell it to stand out.

Knock, knock.
Who's there?
Leaf.
Leaf who?
Leaf me alone - I'm napping!

What do you call a snowman with a six-pack?
An abdominal snowman.

Knock, knock.
Who's there?
Bee.
Bee who?
Bee-lieve it or not, I'm here!

Why did the birthday candle smile?
Because it got to shine.

Why did the tomato turn red?
Because it saw the salad dressing.

What has a bell but isn't a phone?
A bicycle.

Brave balloons borrowed 7 bubbly bears.

How do you make a nap fun?
Dream up something silly.

How do you make a hat feel cool?
Put it on top of the fun.

Knock, knock.
Who's there?
Boo.
Boo who?
I was just saying 'boo' to say hi!

What do you call a star that tells jokes?
A pun-star.

What has a thumb and four fingers but isn't alive?
A glove.

Knock, knock.
Who's there?
Otto.
Otto who?
Otto know if you want to play!

How do you make a sun take a break?
You can't - it always shines.

Why did the cookie sit by the computer?
It wanted a byte.

What do you call a hedgehog that loves to share?
A nice-spine.

What do you call a chicken that tells jokes?
A comedi-hen.

Why did the astronaut eat in outer space?

Because the restaurant had great atmosphere!

Knock, knock.
Who's there?
Cows.
Cows who?
No, cows go 'moo'!

Knock, knock.
Who's there?
Whale.
Whale who?
Whale, whale, whale... look who it is!

What do you call a magician's dog?

A labracadabrador.

Merry milkshakes marched 8 messy monkeys.

How do you make homework disappear?

You don't - you do it fast!

What do you call a cow that just gave birth?

Decalfinated.

Why did the alien go to the party?

It heard it was out of this world.

Peppy pencils packed 8 polite penguins.

How do you make a book feel important?

Put it on the top shelf.

What has a bed but never sleeps?

A river.

How do you make a sandwich laugh?

Tell it something cheesy.

How do you make a penguin sing?

Give it a cool tune to practice.

What do you call a monkey that loves to dance?

A boogie banana.

What do you call a bat that tells jokes?

A pun in the belfry.

What do you call a bee that can't make up its mind?

A maybee.

Knock, knock.
Who's there?
Ketchup.
Ketchup who?
Ketchup with me and let's play!

What do you call a boomerang that comes back with snacks?
A bring-a-rang.

How do you make a cake feel loved?
Give it lots of layers of kindness.

What do you call a belt made of clocks?
A waist of time.

What do you call a cat that loves to chase lasers?
A purr-suer.

I asked a frog for help. He said, 'No problem - I'm hoppy to!'

What do you call a pirate with two eyes and two legs?
A beginner.

What do you call a robot that loves to cook?
A chef-bot.

What do you call a cow that loves movies?

A moo-vie star.

Knock, knock.
Who's there?
Elvis.
Elvis who?
Elvis the door unlocked?

Why did the penguin wear a bowtie?

It was going to a cool party.

I tried to make a joke about paper... but it was tear-able.

Knock, knock.
Who's there?
Dew.
Dew who?
Dew you want to build a snowman?

Knock, knock.
Who's there?
Banana.
Banana who?
Knock, knock.
Who's there?
Banana.
Banana who?
Knock, knock...
Orange you glad I didn't say banana?

What do you call a robot that loves jokes?

A pun-bot.

What do you call an alligator in a vest?

An investigator.

Knock, knock.
Who's there?
Justin.
Justin who?
Justin time!

What do you call a pony with a cough?
A little horse.

I told my hat a joke. It was over its head.

Knock, knock.
Who's there?
Phil.
Phil who?
Phil in the blank: 'open the door'!

Knock, knock.
Who's there?
Interrupting cow.
Interrupting cow wh- MOO!

My calendar is so popular - it's got a date every day.

Why did the cake go to school?
To get a little smarter (and sweeter).

Why did the bed go to school?
To get more rest-education.

Clean clouds counted 5 calm crabs.

Why did the sock feel lonely?

It lost its mate.

Green giraffes glued 6 grumpy geese.

What do you call a cow with two legs?

Lean beef.

Why did the student take a pencil to bed?

To draw the curtains.

Lucky leaves lumbered 5 lazy lions.

What has a tongue but never talks?

A shoe.

Knock, knock.
Who's there?
Bean.
Bean who?
Bean thinking about you!

What kind of bow can't be tied?

A rainbow.

What kind of ship has no captain and no crew?

A friendship.

What do you call a dog that can do magic tricks?

A labracadabrador.

I asked the banana to tell a joke. It split up laughing.

Why did the potato sit by the fire?

It wanted to be a hot potato.

How do you make sneakers faster?

Add speedy laces (and practice!).

Why did the pizza go to music class?

It wanted to learn how to make a good slice of sound.

What kind of cup doesn't hold water?

A cupcake.

Knock, knock.
Who's there?
Pickle.
Pickle who?
Pickle me in - I'm stuck outside!

What do you call a cat that loves chocolate?

A kitty-kat.

Why did the hat sit on the shelf?

It needed some time to cap off the day.

Knock, knock.
Who's there?
Kiwi.
Kiwi who?
Kiwi be friends?

Knock, knock.
Who's there?
Abby.
Abby who?
Abby-thing you want, I can help!

How do you make a door feel welcome?

Give it an open invitation.

What do you call a fox that loves naps?

A doze-fox.

How do you make a classroom quieter?

Whisper your wiggles away.

What do you call a monster that likes to tell jokes?

A pun-ster.

Why did the clock get in trouble?

It kept tocking during quiet time.

Calm crabs camped 6 cheerful clowns.

Why did the car bring a snack?

It didn't want to run out of gas-tro fun.

What do you call a sleeping piece of paper?

A nap-kin.

Knock, knock.
Who's there?
Guess.
Guess who?
You said it!

What do you call a panda that loves bamboo?

A bamboo-fet.

How do you stop a bull from charging?

Take away its credit card.

Why did the carrot get an award?

It was outstanding in the veggie patch.

Why did the mop feel tired?

It had a lot of chores.

What do you call a bear that tells jokes?

A pun-bear-able bear.

What do you call a panda that loves jokes?

A pun-da.

How do you make a lamp feel useful?

Ask it to brighten your day.

Why did the mirror smile?

Because it saw you smiling.

What has many needles but doesn't sew?

A Christmas tree.

How do you make a backpack feel lighter?

Take out the extra rocks (and snacks).

How do you make a spoon and fork get along?

Let them share a plate.

What is at the end of a rainbow?

The letter W.

Knock, knock.
Who's there?
Waddle.
Waddle who?
Waddle you know - I'm a duck!

Why did the computer go to the doctor?

Because it had a virus.

What do you call a bee that loves jokes?

A buzz-kill?
(Nope - a buzz-tickler!)

What do you call a whale that loves school?

A smart-acean.

What do you call an owl who is good at math?

A know-it-owl.

Why did the tennis racket get excited?

It loved a good match.

How do you make a train stop talking?

Tell it to keep its thoughts on track.

I asked the librarian if the library had books on glue. She said, 'They're stuck in the middle!'

Knock, knock.
Who's there?
Abby.
Abby who?
Abby birthday to you!

What gets sharper the more you use it?

Your brain.

What do you call a robot that loves candy?

A sweet-tooth droid.

What do you call a sloth that loves racing?

A slow-motion champion.

What do you call a fish with no eyes?

Fsh.

What do you call a cow with no legs?

Ground beef.

Why did the thunder go to school?

To get a little more striking.

What do you call a kangaroo that can sing?

A pouch performer.

What do you call a robot that loves to play soccer?

A goal-bot.

What has a lot of eyes but can't see?

A potato.

Why did the star go to school?

To get a little brighter.

What runs but never walks?

Water.

What do you call a turtle that loves snacks?

A munchy shell.

Clean crabs cooked 8 cheerful cats.

How do you make a carrot feel heard?

Give it an ear.

What do you call a robot that takes the long way?

R2-Detour.

Why did the student bring string to school?

To tie up loose ends.

Sparkly socks scribbled 4 speedy skateboards.

How do you make a dinosaur smile?

Tell it you're a dino-mite friend.

How do you make an orange relax?

Tell it to juice breathe.

Knock, knock.
Who's there?
Olive.
Olive who?
Olive you and I miss you!

How do you make a snowman feel better?

Give it a warm hug (quick!).

What do you call a cow that is always polite?
Mootiful manners.

What do you call a sleeping penguin?
A snooze-bird.

Cheerful clowns clapped 3 cheerful cookies.

Knock, knock.
Who's there?
Canoe.
Canoe who?
Canoe help me open the door?

What do you call a fish that wears a bowtie?
Sofishticated.

What do you call a bee that is having a bad hair day?
A frizz-bee.

Why did the zebra bring a notebook?
It wanted to keep track of its stripes.

Why did the librarian whisper?
Because the books were sleeping.

Why did the key feel important?

It knew it could unlock the fun.

Why did the egg hide?

It was a little chicken.

Knock, knock.
Who's there?
Nobel.
Nobel who?
No bell - I knocked!

What has hands but can't clap?

A clock.

What do you call a deer with no eyes?

No eye deer.

What do you call a pirate who loves math?

An arrr-ithmetic expert.

Knock, knock.
Who's there?
Olive oil.
Olive oil who?
Olive oil you if you open the door!

Knock, knock.
Who's there?
Harry.
Harry who?
Harry me a snack, please!

Why did the cookie go to school?

To become a smart cookie.

What has cities but no houses, forests but no trees, and water but no fish?

A map.

What do you call a robot that loves music?

A beat-bot.

Why did the lion sit in the sun?

It wanted to feel like the king of the warm jungle.

Knock, knock.
Who's there?
Peas.
Peas who?
Peas let me in!

Knock, knock.
Who's there?
Yoda.
Yoda who?
Yoda best friend!

What do you call a hedgehog that loves hugs?

A cuddle-prickle.

Why did the popcorn feel proud?

It really popped off!

What can you make that no one can see?

A noise.

What comes once in a minute, twice in a moment, but never in a thousand years?

The letter M.

Why did the spoon feel important?

It got to scoop up compliments.

What do you call a funny mountain?

Hill-arious.

What do you call a crab that loves jokes?

A crack-up crab.

What can you hear but not see?

A sound.

Why did the dog bring a pencil?

It wanted to draw a paw-trait.

How do you talk to a giant?

Use big words.

Why did the ice cube feel cool?

Because it was.

Why did the dinosaur bring a toothbrush?

It wanted to brush up on its roar.

Why did the dictionary go to the gym?

To build more definition.

What can you hold without touching it?

Your breath.

Woolly waffles waved 7 wide whales.

How do you keep an astronaut baby from crying?

You rocket.

What do you call a frog that loves music?

A ribbit-and-roll star.

What do you call a squirrel with a great memory?

A nut-ebook.

How do you make a bicycle helmet happy?

Give it a head to help.

Why did the monkey like bananas?

Because they were appealing.

What has a cap but no head?

A bottle.

Why did the scissors run away?

They couldn't handle the pressure.

How do you make a broom feel fancy?

Give it a little bow tie.

Knock, knock.
Who's there?
Broken pencil.
Broken pencil who?
Never mind - it's pointless.

Knock, knock.
Who's there?
Nanna.
Nanna who?
Nanna your jokes are the best!

Why did the pizza sit on the roof?

It wanted to be on top of the pie.

Muddy mice mooned 4 mysterious milkshakes.

Why did the orange stop rolling?

It ran out of juice.

I gave my friend a pencil with two erasers. He said, 'That's pointless!'

What kind of room do ghosts avoid?

The living room.

How do you make a lunchbox feel excited?

Pack a surprise note (in your head - no writing needed!).

Why did the robot sit quietly?

It was processing a pun.

What do you call a sleeping car?

A car-napper.

Why did the sun bring sunglasses?

Because it was shining so bright!

Tiny trains tiptoed 3 tropical tacos.

Why did the pencil sharpener laugh?

It was on point.

How do you make an astronaut wave?

Give them space to do it.

Why did the tree go to the dentist?

It needed a root canal.

Why did the calculator feel useful?

People could always count on it.

Knock, knock.
Who's there?
Water.
Water who?
Water you waiting for? Open up!

Why did the clown bring a ruler?

To measure the giggles.

Why did the bicycle wear a helmet?

It wanted to stay safe and sound.

What do you call a giraffe that loves jokes?

A tall tale teller.

Why did the toaster blush?

It got toasted by a compliment.

Knock, knock.
Who's there?
Dishes.
Dishes who?
Dishes a nice door you have!

Lucky lemons lumbered 3 lazy lions.

How do you make a zebra easy to spot?

Don't - it's already striped!

Knock, knock.
Who's there?
Noah.
Noah who?
Noah way I'm leaving without a cookie!

What do you call a monster who loves dancing?

The boogie man.

Knock, knock.
Who's there?
Fig.
Fig who?
Fig-ure out who it is - it's me!

Knock, knock.
Who's there?
Kanga.
Kanga who?
Kanga-ratulations - you opened the door!

I gave my friend a map.
He said, 'This really helps me get my bearings!'

Knock, knock.
Who's there?
Tank.
Tank who?
You're welcome!

Knock, knock.
Who's there?
Al.
Al who?
Al give you a hint - open the door!

Why did the book go to the doctor?

It had a bad case of the spine-aches.

Knock, knock.
Who's there?
Luke.
Luke who?
Luke through the peephole and find out!

I tried to tell a joke about a bed... but I couldn't make it up.

Why did the pillow win an award?

It was outstanding in its comfort field.

How do you make a mirror laugh?

Smile at it first.

Clean clowns colored 6 crazy clouds.

Knock, knock.
Who's there?
Donut.
Donut who?
Donut forget to smile today!

How do you make a spoon feel like a superhero?

Call it Captain Scoop.

How do you make a pencil feel brave?

Remind it it's got a good point.

Knock, knock.
Who's there?
Boo-tiful.
Boo-tiful who?
Boo-tiful day, isn't it?

What do you call a robot that loves homework?

A study-bot.

Knock, knock.
Who's there?
Annie.
Annie who?
Annie-body home?

Knock, knock.
Who's there?
Adore.
Adore who?
Adore-ably, I'm here!

What do you call a shark that loves jokes?

A laugh-fin.

What has a ring but isn't jewelry?

A telephone.

How do you make a sheep say 'wow'?

Show it a baa-mazing trick.

Why did the duck bring soap?

It wanted to quack up clean.

How do you make a bed feel cozy?

Tuck it in with blankets.

What has two legs but can't walk?

A pair of pants.

Knock, knock.
Who's there?
Moo.
Moo who?
Moo-ve over, I'm coming in!

Knock, knock.
Who's there?
Lettuce.
Lettuce who?
Lettuce in - we brought pizza!

Why did the lightning get a medal?
It was electrifying.

What do you call a dog that loves to nap?
A snooze hound.

My penguin friend loves jokes.
He's always cracking up.

What do you call a rhino that loves parties?
A horn-raiser.

What do you call a vampire who loves baseball?
A bat boy.

How do you make a watermelon laugh?
Tell it a seedy joke.

Why did the stadium get so hot?
Because all the fans left!

What do you call a dinosaur that crashes his car?

A Tyrannosaurus wreck.

Knock, knock.
Who's there?
Doris.
Doris who?
Doris locked - that's why I'm knocking!

What kind of room has no doors or windows?

A mushroom.

Dapper donuts dropped 6 delightful ducks.

What do you call a cow that plays an instrument?

A moo-sician.

What has one head, one foot, and four legs?

A bed.

Knock, knock.
Who's there?
Ice cream.
Ice cream who?
Ice cream so you can hear me!

What do you call a snail that tells jokes?

A slow comedian.

What do you call a pile of cats?

A meow-ntain.

Knock, knock.
Who's there?
Wanda.
Wanda who?
Wanda go to the playground with me?

How do you greet a shark?

With a big wave from far away.

What do you call a robot that loves pizza?

A slice-bot.

Why did the watermelon jump into the lake?

It wanted to be a water-melon.

What has a bark but no bite?

A tree.

Knock, knock.
Who's there?
Peanut.
Peanut who?
Peanut butter open the door!

What do you call a dinosaur that loves to sing?

A rap-tor.

Tough tigers tested 7 ticklish trombones.

Knock, knock.
Who's there?
Dora.
Dora who?
Dora the door open, please!

Why did the cat sit on the computer?

It wanted to keep an eye on the mouse.

What can you keep after giving it to someone?

Your word.

How do you make a pirate share?

Say, 'Arrr you ready to be kind?'

I asked the cloud to move. It said, 'I'm just going through a phase.'

Knock, knock.
Who's there?
A little old lady.
A little old lady who?
I didn't know you could yodel!

What do you call a walrus that loves the beach?

A sand-walrus.

Why did the fish bring a pencil?

To draw some fin-tastic pictures.

What do you call a fake noodle?

An impasta.

Mellow muffins mooned 5 mysterious monkeys.

What do you call a dog that loves to swim?

A pup-perfish.

What do you call a dinosaur taking a nap?

A dino-snooze.

Knock, knock.
Who's there?
Iva.
Iva who?
Iva got a surprise for you!

What do you call a rabbit that tells secrets?

A whisper-hare.

What has many pages but isn't a book?

A calendar.

Why did the music note go to school?

To get better at scales.

Knock, knock.
Who's there?
Noodle.
Noodle who?
Noodle-ly, I'm hungry!

What do you call a snowman in summer?

A puddle.

Bossy bunnies bounced 7 bright balloons.

Why did the orange go to school?

To become a little zest-ier.

What do you call a rabbit that loves carrots?

A crunch-bunny.

What do you call a fish that keeps a secret?

A clam.

Why did the banana wear a cape?

It was a super peel-er.

What do you call a hippo that loves to dance?
A hip-hoppo.

How do you make a sock feel less lonely?
Find its missing mate.

How do you make a bathtub sing?
Add bubbles for backup vocals.

My notebook is a great singer. It always hits the right notes.

Why did the giraffe get good at basketball?
It had a great reach.

What do you call a cat with eight legs?
An octo-puss.

Why did the kite stop talking?
It got tongue-tied in the wind.

How do you get a baby alien to sleep?
Sing a lullaby from another galaxy.

What do you call a crab that plays baseball?

A pinch hitter.

What do you call a space dog?

An astro-mutt.

What do you call a cat who loves to bowl?

An alley cat.

Why did the notebook smile?

It had everything written down.

What do you call a pig that takes a bath?

Clean bacon.

What do you call a fish that sings?

A tuna.

What do you call an elephant that doesn't matter?

An irrelephant.

What is black and white and read all over?

A newspaper.

Knock, knock.
Who's there?
Broccoli.
Broccoli who?
Broccoli doesn't have a door - I do!

I told my shoes a secret. Now they're tied up in it.

What do you call a sleeping bull?
A bulldozer.

Wiggly whales whirled 4 whispery waffles.

Why did the door get a high-five?
It was always open to new ideas.

Why did the bear bring honey to the picnic?
Because it had a sweet tooth.

What do you call a cat that loves to nap?
A purr-napper.

I tried to tell a joke about a trampoline...
but I kept bouncing around.

How do you make a fish giggle?

Tell it something finny.

What do you call a dinosaur that loves to sleep late?

A snooze-a-saurus.

Knock, knock.
Who's there?
Figs.
Figs who?
Figs the doorbell - it's broken!

Funny fireflies flew 5 fuzzy flowers.

I told a joke to the elevator. It took it to another level.

Knock, knock.
Who's there?
Harry.
Harry who?
Harry good book lately?

Why did the dinosaur carry a backpack?

It had a lot of dino-stuff to do.

My dog asked for a snack. It was a real treat-ment plan.

Dapper dogs daydreamed 5 dainty dinosaurs.

What do you call a dog that loves to play in mud?

A dirty pup.

Why did the fork get a medal?

It always stuck with it.

Why did the trophy smile?

It got a big hand.

Why did the vampire read the newspaper?

To keep up with the current events.

Knock, knock.
Who's there?
Ho-ho.
Ho-ho who?
You know - Santa!

What do you call a pencil that won a race?

The write winner.

Knock, knock.
Who's there?
Noah.
Noah who?
Noah good place like home!

What is easy to lift but hard to throw?

A feather.

Why did the taco wear a sweater?

It didn't want to be chili.

What do you call a spider that loves the internet?

A web designer.

Why did the robot bring a broom?

It wanted to sweep the floor-bots.

What begins with T, ends with T, and has T in it?

A teapot.

Why did the student bring a flashlight to class?

To have a bright idea.

Why did the soap feel proud?

It cleaned up its act.

How do you make a cookie feel confident?

Remind it it's one smart cookie.

What do you call a deer with no eyes and no legs?

Still no eye deer.

How do you make a bear stop grumbling?

Give it a honey of a compliment.

How do you make a dragon behave?

You don't - you just offer snacks.

Knock, knock.
Who's there?
Butter.
Butter who?
Butter hurry - I'm melting!

Why did the rain bring a trumpet?

It wanted to make a big splash.

Sticky snakes sipped 8 sticky snowmen.

Knock, knock.
Who's there?
Mustache.
Mustache who?
I mustache you a question!

Knock, knock.
Who's there?
Tuna.
Tuna who?
Tuna in tomorrow - today I'm busy!

Why did the broom get a trophy?

It swept the competition.

What do you call a kangaroo that loves music?

A hip-hop-roo.

How do you make a paperclip feel proud?

Tell it it's holding everything together.

How do you make a ruler feel confident?

Tell it it always measures up.

Knock, knock.
Who's there?
Radar.
Radar who?
Radar you going to open the door?

Knock, knock.
Who's there?
Alpaca.
Alpaca who?
Alpaca the snacks - you pack the games!

Knock, knock.
Who's there?
Annie.
Annie who?
Annie-thing for a laugh!

Why did the student sit on the clock?

Because they wanted to be on time.

Messy marbles marched 7 messy magicians.

How do you make a plate feel fancy?
Give it a royal serving.

How do you make a key feel important?
Tell it it's the key to success.

What do you call a rabbit with fleas?
Bugs Bunny.

What do you call a wolf that sings?
A howl-star.

What do you call a pirate's favorite letter?
You'd think it's R,
but it's the C!

Purple penguins popped 3 proud pizzas.

Knock, knock.
Who's there?
Zero.
Zero who?
Zero problem -
I'm just saying hi!

Why did the crab never share its snacks?
Because it was a little shellfish.

Why did the wind laugh?
It was tickled by the leaves.

What has a head but no brain?
A cabbage.

How do you make broccoli feel cool?
Tell it it's a little tree superstar.

What do you call a lazy kangaroo?
A pouch potato.

What do you call a dinosaur with a big vocabulary?
A thesaurus.

What do you call a dinosaur that writes stories?
A dino-author.

What can be cracked, made, told, and played?
A joke.

How do you make a dictionary feel needed?

Ask it to look up something silly.

Knock, knock.
Who's there?
Sue.
Sue who?
Sue-per happy to see you!

What do you call a bear with no teeth?

A gummy bear.

How do you make glue feel happy?

Let it stick around with friends.

Knock, knock.
Who's there?
Nanna.
Nanna who?
Nanna your business - open up!

What has lots of teeth but can't bite?

A comb.

What do you call a ghost who tells jokes?

A silly spirit.

Why did the painter sit near the window?

It wanted a better view to draw.

How do you make a dog stop barking in class?

Give it a paws button.

Why did the bee bring a backpack?

It had a lot of buzz-iness to carry.

What do you call a dog that tells jokes?

A punny pup.

Gentle grapes glued 8 green ghosts.

Why did the snail carry a suitcase?

It was ready for a slow trip.

My crayons quit their job. They were tired of being colored in.

How do you make a notebook less nervous?

Tell it to take notes and breathe.

What do you call a ghost's favorite dessert?

I-scream.

What has a zipper but no mouth?

A jacket.

Why did the dog sit in the shade?

Because it didn't want to be a hot dog.

What kind of ball doesn't bounce?

A snowball.

How do you make a knight laugh?

Tell it a pun in shining armor.

I asked the pencil sharpener for a joke. It said, 'I'm on point!'

Why did the frog take the bus?

His car got toad away.

What do you call a fox that loves to read?

A clever chapter-fox.

What do you call a fox in a bakery?

A sneaky snacker.

Why did the piano sit quietly?

It was waiting for the right key moment.

What do you call a robot who tells great jokes?

A laugh-o-matic.

Dusty daisies dashed 6 dapper drums.

Knock, knock.
Who's there?
Orange.
Orange who?
Orange you going to let me in?

What do you call a robot that loves to clean?

A tidy-bot.

Why did the soccer ball stop talking?

It got kicked out of the conversation.

Knock, knock.
Who's there?
Ya.
Ya who?
No thanks, I use the doorbell.

Knock, knock.
Who's there?
Oreo.
Oreo who?
Oreo you going to open this door?

Loopy lions lifted 5 lovely ladybugs.

Fast foxes folded 9 fierce fries.

What do you call a frog in a fancy restaurant?

A frogette.

Why did the student eat the homework?

Because the teacher said it was a piece of cake!

How do you make a robot dance?

Press the boogie button.

Why did the witch bring a broom to school?

It didn't want to miss the bus.

Knock, knock.
Who's there?
Yacht.
Yacht who?
Yacht to let me in - I'm freezing!

Bossy bananas built 9 bossy books.

How do you make a star feel famous?

Ask for its autograph (in your imagination!).

What kind of key opens a banana?

A mon-key.

What do you call a cat that loves to tell stories?

A purr-teller.